Woodland Wildlife

Grey Squirrels

by G. G. Lake

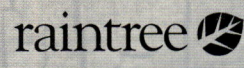
raintree
a Capstone company — publishers for children

Pebble® Plus

Raintree is an imprint of Capstone Global Library Limited, a company incorporated in England and Wales having its registered office at 264 Banbury Road, Oxford, OX2 7DY – Registered company number: 6695582

www.raintree.co.uk
myorders@raintree.co.uk

Edited by Gena Chester
Designed by Juliette Peters
Picture research by Wanda Winch
Production by Steve Walker

ISBN 978 1 4747 2185 1
20 19 18 17 16
10 9 8 7 6 5 4 3 2 1

British Library Cataloguing in Publication Data
A full catalogue record for this book is available from the British Library.

Acknowledgements
We would like to thank the following for permission to reproduce photographs: Alamy: FLPA, 11; Minden Pictures: Stephen Dalton, 5; Shutterstock: alicedaniel, illustrated forest items, Anna Subbotina, 22–23, AR Pictures, tree bark design, Bob Orsillo, 7, Dom1530, 21, elina, 24, Emi, 9 (top), gdvcom, 13, Heiko Kiera, 15, lightpoet, 19, Maciej Olszewski, cover, mythja, 1, P.Preeda, 17, Stawek, 9 (map), Sunny Forest, 3.

Every effort has been made to contact copyright holders of material reproduced in this book. Any omissions will be rectified in subsequent printings if notice is given to the publisher.

All the Internet addresses (URLs) given in this book were valid at the time of going to press. However, due to the dynamic nature of the Internet, some addresses may have changed, or sites may have changed or ceased to exist since publication. While the author and publisher regret any inconvenience this may cause readers, no responsibility for any such changes can be accepted by either the author or the publisher.

Printed and bound in China.

Contents

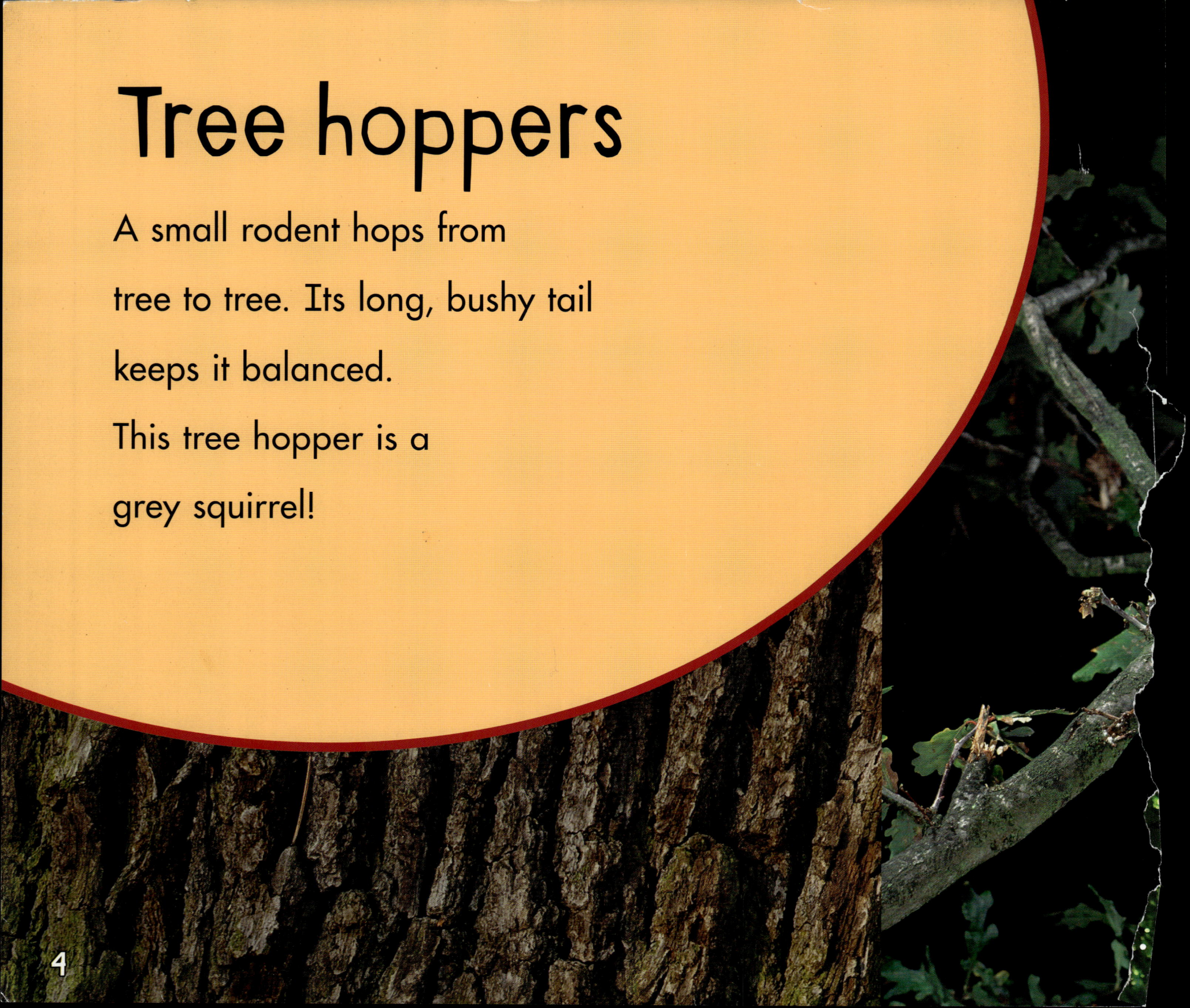

Tree hoppers

A small rodent hops from tree to tree. Its long, bushy tail keeps it balanced. This tree hopper is a grey squirrel!

Grey squirrels have grey or sometimes black fur. Parts of their coats can be brown. Sometimes their bellies are white.

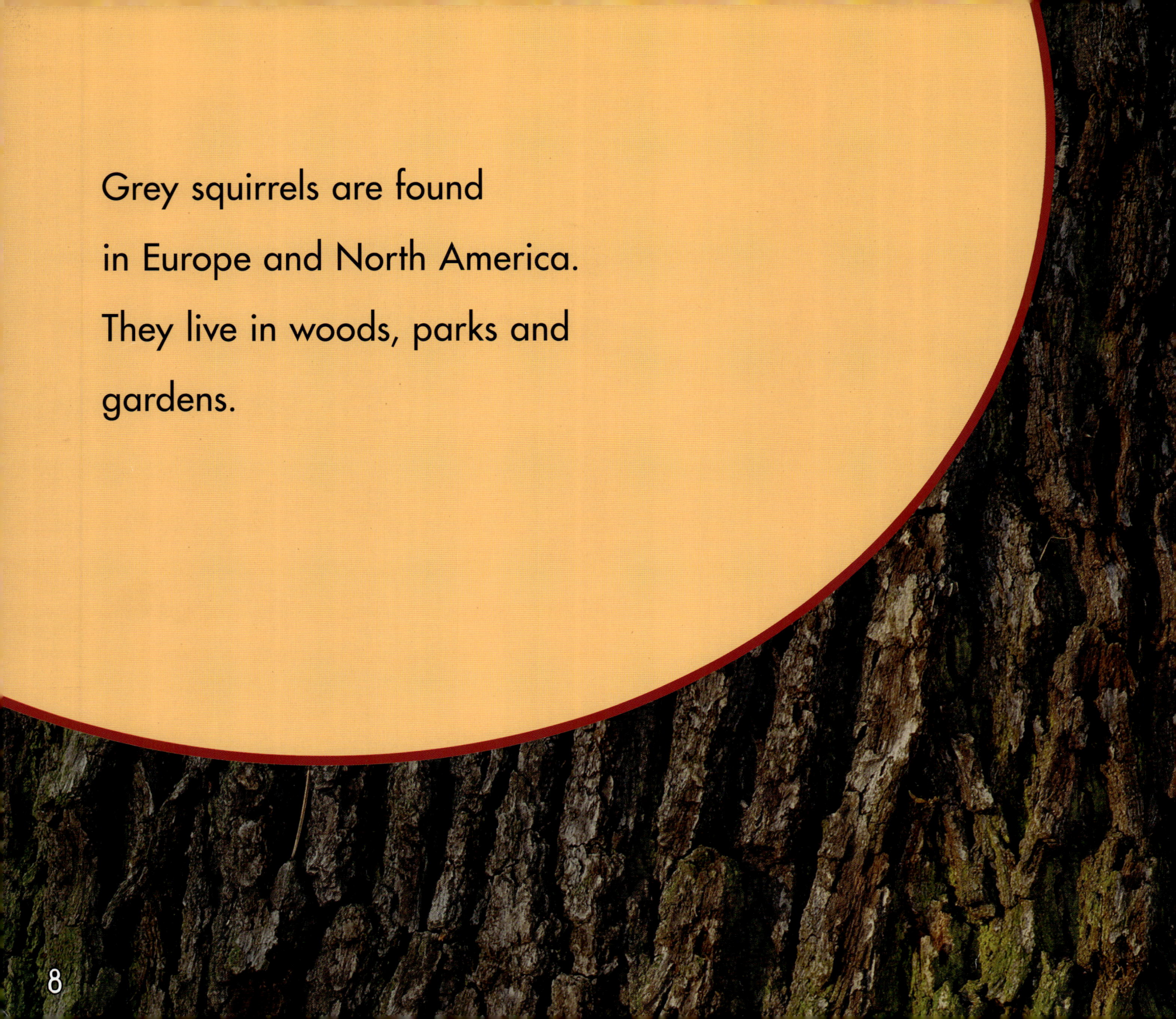

Grey squirrels are found
in Europe and North America.
They live in woods, parks and
gardens.

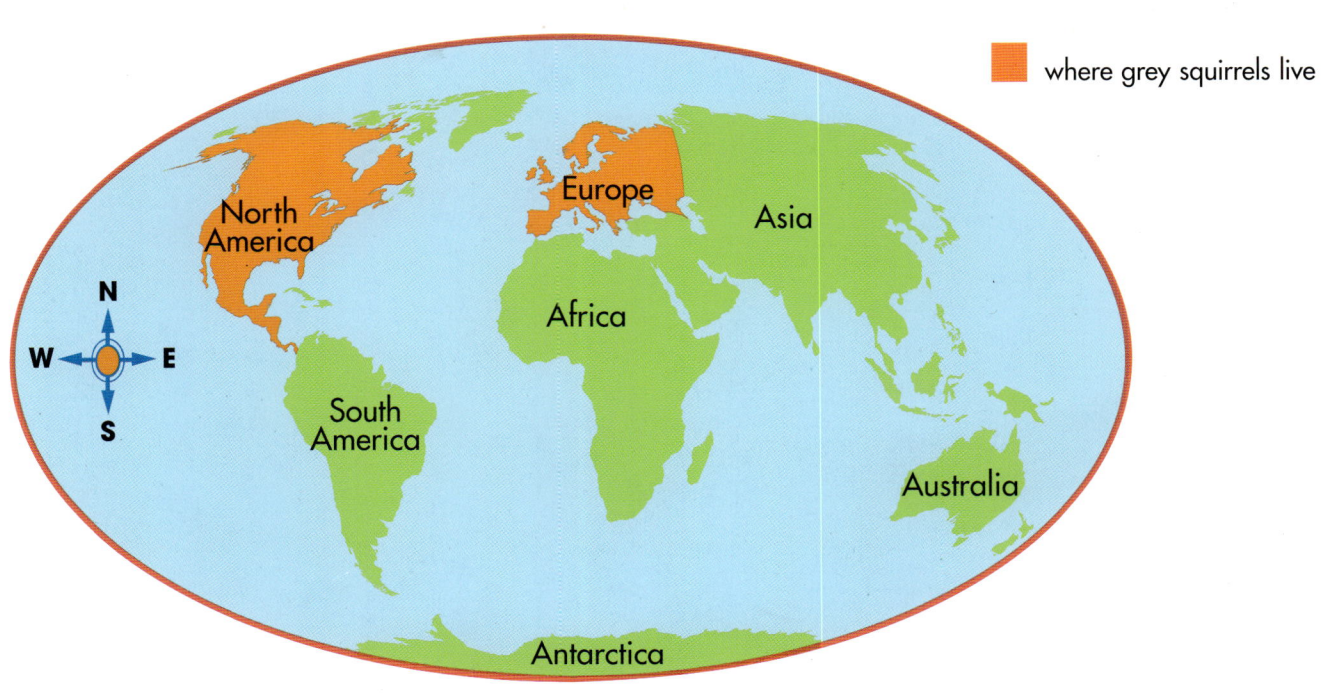

■ where grey squirrels live

North
America

Europe

Asia

Africa

South
America

Australia

Antarctica

N
W E
S

Woodland homes

Grey squirrel homes are called dreys and dens. Dreys are built high up in tree branches. They are made of leaves and sticks.

Squirrels live in dens in winter.

Dens are found in hollow trees.

Squirrels stay warm inside dens.

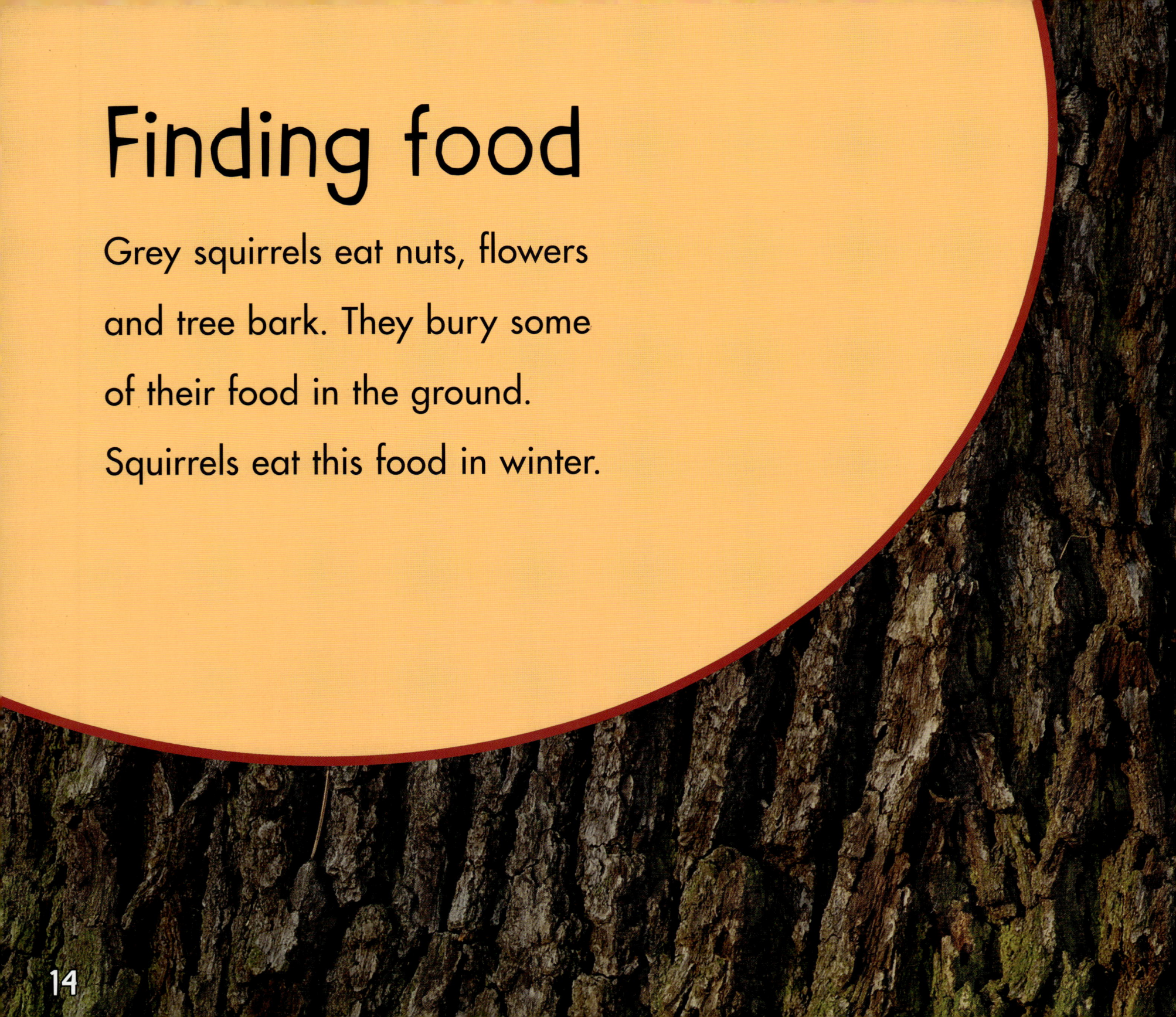

Finding food

Grey squirrels eat nuts, flowers and tree bark. They bury some of their food in the ground. Squirrels eat this food in winter.

Staying safe

Squirrels have a lot of predators.
Foxes, weasels and hawks hunt
them. Grey squirrels stay close
to their homes to keep safe.

Sometimes grey squirrels outrun predators. Their back legs are powerful. Grey squirrels can run up to 32 kilometres (20 miles) per hour.

Baby Squirrels

Female squirrels have two to eight babies twice a year. Babies stay with their mothers for two to three months. Then the young squirrels are ready to leave the drey.

Glossary

balance keep steady and not fall over

bark hard covering of a tree

den inside of a tree trunk where wild animals may live

drey home of squirrels; dreys are found in tree branches

fur thick hair that covers an animal

hollow empty inside

hunt find and catch animals for food

predator animal that hunts other animals for food

rodent mammal with long front teeth used for gnawing; rats, mice and squirrels are rodents

wood large area covered with trees and plants

Read more

Look Inside a Tree (Look Inside a...), Richard and Louise Spilsbury (Raintree, 2014)

A Nature Walk in the Woods (Nature Walks), Louise and Richard Spilsbury (Raintree, 2015)

Squirrel (City Safari), Isabel Thomas (Raintree, 2014)

Websites

www.bbc.co.uk/nature/life/Eastern_gray_squirrel
Watch videos of grey squirrels in action.

www.rspb.org.uk/makeahomeforwildlife/wildlifegarden/
atoz/g/greysquirrel.aspx
Find out about the squirrels in your garden!

www.wildlifetrusts.org/species/grey-squirrel
Find out more about grey squirrels, including when and where to spot them!

Comprehension questions

1. What does the word hollow mean?

2. How long do baby squirrels stay with their mother?

3. Where in the world do grey squirrels live?

Index